OVER, UNDER, IN, AND OUCH!

by Trudy Harris

Illustrated by Steve Haskamp

The Millbrook Press
Brookfield, Connecticut

Text copyright © 2003 by Trudy Harris
Illustrations copyright © 2003 by Steve Haskamp
All rights reserved

Reading Consultant: Lea M. McGee

Silly Millies and the Silly Millies logo are trademarks
of The Millbrook Press, Inc.

Library of Congress Cataloging-in-Publication Data
Harris, Trudy.
Over, under, in, and ouch! / Trudy Harris;
illustrated by Steve Haskamp.
p. cm. — (Silly Millies)
Summary: Rhyming advice about some
silly problems introduces the use of prepositions.
ISBN 0-7613-2912-9 (lib. bdg.) — ISBN 0-7613-1946-8 (pbk.)
[1. Dogs—Fiction. 2. English language—Prepositions—Fiction.
3. Stories in rhyme.] I. Haskamp, Steve, ill. II. Title. III. Series.
PZ8.3.H24318Ov 2003   [E]—dc21   2003002217

Published by The Millbrook Press
2 Old New Milford Road
Brookfield, Connecticut 06804
www.millbrookpress.com

Printed in the United States of America
5 4 3 2 1 (lib.)
5 4 3 2 1 (pbk.)

OVER, UNDER, IN, AND OUCH!

If your brother conks his head
jumping under the fence,
you can help poor Rover.

SUPER
FRISBEE DOG

Just tell him, "Jump . . .
OVER!"

When rain soaks your hair
with your umbrella low,
give this a try:

Hold the umbrella . . .

HIGH.

If your feet get wet and chilly
when you muddle through a puddle,
here's a tip that I have found:

Next time, walk . . .
AROUND.

Don't smear jelly for your sandwich
on the outside of your bread.

To keep your paws clean,
spread the jelly . . .
in BETWEEN.

If your goldfish flips and flops
until he plops
out of his bowl,

grab him by the fin,
and gently drop him . . .
IN.

When you drop a shiny nickel,
don't search high
up in the sky.

The nickel fell, you know,
so it is likely . . .
LOW.

If sticky globs of pudding
drip and drizzle
by your mouth,
next time, open wide
and put the spoon . . .
INSIDE.

Don't walk toward
an angry swarm
of stinging, buzzing bees.

If you see a hive, don't stay.
Turn around and run . . .
AWAY.

With mountains of garbage
piled high in your house,

don't stand there and shout.

Instead, take it . . .

OUT.

If a dirty bird drops doo-doo on your head, don't look below.

That sneaky rotten dove
is probably . . .
ABOVE.

While you lie on your quilt,
do you shiver and shake?
Well, no wonder.
It's much warmer . . .
UNDER.

If your coat sleeves look strange
hanging over your arms,
here's what you do:

You stick your arms . . .
THROUGH.

With his head at the bottom,
your snowman will fall.

So he won't go "Ker-plop,"
stack his head on the . . .
TOP.

At the back of this book, if you
still want more fun,
here's where to hunt:
Turn again to the . . .
FRONT.

Dear Parents:
Congratulations! By sharing this book with
your child, you are taking an important step in
helping him or her become a good reader. *Over,
Under, In, and Ouch!* is perfect for the child who
is beginning to read alone. Below are some ideas
for making sure your child's reading experience
is a positive one.

Tips for Reading

- First, read the book aloud to your child. Then, if your child is able
  to "sound out" the words, invite him or her to read to you. If your
  child is unsure about a word you can help by asking, "What word
  do you think it might be?" or, "Does that make sense?" Point to
  the first letter or two of the word and ask your child to make that
  sound. If she or he is stumped, read the word slowly, pointing to
  each letter as you sound them out. Always provide lots of praise
  for the hard work your child is doing.
- If your child knows the words but is having trouble reading aloud,
  cut a plain white ruler-sized strip of paper to place under the line
  as your child reads. This will help your child keep track of his or
  her place.
- If your child is a beginning reader, have her or him read this book
  aloud to you. Reading and rereading is the best way to help any
  child become a successful reader.

Tips for Discussion

- In every picture of this book there are other things that illustrate
  the position word being used. Did you find them all?
- Instead of using people to illustrate this book, the artist used dogs.
  Could he have used fish? What about using a non-living thing,
  like buildings? Why wouldn't that be as much fun?
- Have fun thinking of word pairs. Can you think of more
  prepositions? Think of words that describe emotions.

Lea M. McGee, Ed.D.
Professor, Literacy Education
University of Alabama